W9-BRS-540

MY FIRST LOOK AT SCIENCE

LIGHT FROM THE SUN CAN MAKE RAINBOWS

Light

MELISSA GISH

CREATIVE EDUCATION

Published by Creative Education

123 South Broad Street, Mankato, Minnesota 56001

Creative Education is an imprint of The Creative Company

Designed by Rita Marshall

Photographs by Corbis (Tibor Bognár, Ralph A. Clevenger, Pat Doyle, Japack Company, Layne Kennedy, Lester Lefkowitz, Danny Lehman, Pete Saloutos), Getty Images (Dennis Flaherty, Nicholas Rigg)

Cover illustration © 1996 Roberto Innocenti

Copyright © 2006 Creative Education

International copyright reserved in all countries. No part of this book may be reproduced in any form without written permission from the publisher.

Printed in the United States of America

Library of Congress Cataloging-in-Publication Data

Gish, Melissa. Light / by Melissa Gish.

p. cm. — (My first look at science)

Includes index.

ISBN 1-58341-373-1

1. Light—Juvenile literature. 2. Optics—Juvenile literature. I. Title. II. Series.

QC360.G57 2005   535—dc22   2004055261

First edition 9 8 7 6 5 4 3 2 1

LIGHT

Everything Needs Light

All living things need light from the sun. The biggest trees need light to grow. The smallest lizards need light to stay warm on cold days. Even people need to spend some time in the sun to be healthy.

Some places on Earth are very dark. The bottom of the sea is dark. But fish that live there count on light, too. That's because they eat things that grow in the sunlight.

Sunlight makes shallow water warm

WAVES OF LIGHT

Light is a kind of energy. It travels over paths called light waves. Each color of the rainbow is a different light wave. Without light, there would be no color.

When objects are really hot, they send out light waves. Fire sends out light waves that are orange or red. **Natural gas** sends out light waves that are blue.

Sunlight shines through
clear glass, but it
bounces off of mirrors.

LIGHT BRINGS OUT THIS FOREST'S GREEN COLOR

Not all light waves are bright or colorful. Some are **invisible** to people. They still affect us, though. They can give us a sunburn or make us feel hot.

COLORED LIGHT

Sunlight does not seem to have any color. We call it white light. But sunlight is really a mix of all colors. Light from the sun makes every color on Earth.

Plants change light
waves into food.
Almost all plants
need sunlight to grow.

PLANTS GROW DURING THE SUNNY SUMMER

Special pieces of glass called lenses can break white light into separate colors. Drops of rain are like little lenses. They break up sunlight. This is what makes a rainbow.

When light hits something, some of the light is **absorbed**. Some of it is **reflected**. This gives things the color we see. When light hits a plant, every light color except green gets absorbed. Only green bounces back to our eyes.

Light travels in a straight line.

Pieces of glass can "bend"

light and make it

go different directions.

DROPS OF RAIN CAN BREAK UP SUNLIGHT

Light in Our Homes

Light travels very, very fast. When you turn on a light switch, the light seems to fill the room instantly. Your eyes cannot see light as it travels.

Light bulbs have little wires inside them. The wires get hot and glow. This sends out light waves. A light bulb is like a tiny sun. It makes white light.

WIRES GLOW INSIDE A LIGHT BULB

Some lights are shaped like long tubes. They are called **fluorescent** lights. Fluorescent lights do not make pure white light. Sometimes the light is pale blue or purple.

THE SUN'S LIGHT USUALLY LOOKS WHITE

The sun has been sending light to Earth for a long, long time. In dark places or at night, we use light bulbs or flashlights to see. All life on Earth needs light to grow. And light is what makes our world warm and colorful!

Light does not go

around things.

If something blocks the light,

a shadow is made.

IT FEELS COOLER TO STAND IN A SHADOW

Hands-on: The Color Spectrum

You can break sunlight into different colors with this experiment.

What You Need

A small mirror

A piece of white paper

Water

A cake pan

What You Do

1. Fill the pan about half full with water.
2. Put the pan in the sun.
3. Hold the mirror underwater with one hand. Hold the piece of paper in your other hand.
4. Tip the mirror and paper so that sunlight bounces from the mirror onto the paper. You will see the sunlight broken into lines of seven different colors. This is called the color spectrum!

LIGHT CAN BEND TO SHOW THE COLOR SPECTRUM

Index

Words to Know

absorbed—pulled in; water is absorbed by a towel

fluorescent—a kind of light that comes in a long tube

invisible—something that you cannot see, even though it is there

natural gas—gas like air that is burned to make heat

reflected—bounced back; when you look in a mirror, your face is reflected

Read More

Branley, Franklyn M. *Day Light, Night Light: Where Light Comes From*. New York: HarperTrophy, 1998.

Challoner, Jack. *Light and Dark*. Austin, Tex.: Raintree Steck-Vaughn, 1997.

Robson, Pam. *Light, Color & Lenses*. New York: Shooting Star Press, 1995.

Explore the Web

Science of Light http://www.surfnetkids.com/optics.htm

The Light Education Page http://www.lightwave.soton.ac.uk

Optics for Kids http://www.opticsforkids.org